Campbell's

Weeknight
COOKING

Weeknight
COOKING

pil

Publications
International, Ltd.

Favorite Brand Name Recipes at www.:

Special thanks to the Campbell's Kitchen, Lucinda Ayers, Vice President, and Catherine Marschean-Spivak, Group Manager.

Photography on pages 9, 11, 13, 17, 29, 31, 45, 47, 61, 63, 65, 67, 79, 81 and 87 by Stephen Hamilton Photographics, Inc., Chicago.

Pictured on the front cover: Chicken & Broccoli Alfredo *(page 8)*.
Pictured on the back cover (clockwise from top): Baked Pork Chops with Garden Stuffing *(page 60)*, Savory Vegetable Stuffing Bake *(page 80)* and Chicken Cacciatore *(page 44)*.

ISBN-13: 978-1-4127-9084-0
ISBN-10: 1-4127-9084-0

Manufactured in China.

8 7 6 5 4 3 2 1

Microwave Cooking: Microwave ovens vary in wattage. Use the cooking times as guidelines and check for doneness before adding more time.

Preparation/Cooking Times: Preparation times are based on the approximate amount of time required to assemble the recipe before cooking, baking, chilling or serving. These times include preparation steps such as measuring, chopping and mixing. The fact that some preparations and cooking can be done simultaneously is taken into account. Preparation of optional ingredients and serving suggestions is not included.

contents

44

66

78

WELCOME TO

Weeknight Cooking

with Campbell's®

When Campbell Soup Company learned in 1916 that consumers were using our soups as ingredients and not just as an integral part of a meal, we began to provide recipes aimed at helping them get dinner on the table in simple and delicious ways.

Over the years, however, life took a turn— a turn into the fast lane—and bringing the family together for dinner every night after working a full day now takes commitment, planning, organization and a little inspiration. And a few meal ideas and recipes wouldn't hurt, either.

Throughout this cookbook, you will find recipes that are perfect for weeknight dinners: They're familiar dishes that families love; they're easy to prepare; they don't use a lot of ingredients; and the ingredients are familiar and can be found in any supermarket.

Now for the planning and the organization

Get Organized

Planning meals for the week doesn't have to be a difficult, time-consuming activity. If selecting a specific recipe for each day of the week is too daunting, decide on a general theme for each day of the week: For instance, Monday could be soup night; Tuesday could be casserole night; Wednesday, pasta; Thursday, chicken,

and so on. Then fit recipes into each theme.

Next, decide on side dishes, salads and breads for each meal and select recipes for them. Or, keep these general as well: a deli salad with soup on Monday, a bagged green salad with Tuesday's casserole, garlic bread and a steamed vegetable with the pasta on Wednesday.

From the recipes or general themes, compile a shopping list. Aim to shop for one week of meals at a time. Keeping a well-stocked pantry is key to getting dinner on the table in the evening.

Get Inspired

Most cooks have a repertoire of recipes for several basic dishes that they use most of the time: soups, casseroles, stir-fries, burgers, pizza, pasta, meat loaf, and so on. You can keep these dishes interesting by finding ways to vary them from time to time. Here are some suggestions:

■ **Jazz up soup:** If you plan to serve Campbell's® Tomato Soup, change it up with Pepperidge Farm® Croutons and/or shredded cheese. Make pizza soup by stirring in shredded mozzarella cheese, pepperoni slices, and oregano. For taco soup, stir in salsa and sour cream, and then top with shredded cheese and crumbled tortilla chips. Or, have a soup buffet: Heat up one or more varieties of Campbell's® soup, and set up a buffet of toppings.

■ Try turkey: Substitute ground turkey for ground beef in burgers, meat loaf, chili, and casseroles.

■ Season with soup: Use Campbell's® cream soups, Swanson® broths, and Pace® salsa to add exciting flavors to pork chops, chicken, stir-fries and shrimp as they cook. Campbell's® Chunky™ Chili is the perfect topper for a variety of dishes, including nachos and hot dogs.

■ Pick your pasta: Vary the type of pasta you use in casseroles. Substitute penne for macaroni, for example. For pasta night, buy quick-cooking fresh pasta instead of dried. It's available in many shapes and flavors in the refrigerated section of the supermarket. Shredded mozzarella cheese may be the traditional choice to top most pasta dishes, but Cheddar, Parmesan, provolone, and Mexican-flavored cheeses will bring a whole new taste to your pasta and casserole recipes.

■ Veg out: Add thawed, frozen vegetables to pizza and meat loaf. Frozen vegetables cook faster and keep longer than fresh, so keep them on hand for a variety of uses.

Get Cooking

Good cooking doesn't have to mean hours of prep work and slaving over a hot stove. Try these ideas:

■ Organize your kitchen: Keep cutting boards near the sink, and store knives on the counter or in a drawer near the cutting boards. Keep utensils in a container next to the stove or in a drawer nearby.

■ Organize your pantry: Keep canned and jarred goods together, grains on the same shelf, and oils within easy reach. Find a system that works for you.

■ Deli for dinner: Stop by the supermarket deli for cut-up vegetables, salad fixings, rotisserie chicken and prepared salads.

■ Quick fix: Use prepared foods such as Campbell's® soups, Swanson® broths, Prego® pasta sauces, bags of salad and greens, shredded cabbage for slaw and refrigerated mashed potatoes.

■ Keep it simple: Simply prepared foods can make some of the best meals. For instance, cook thinner cuts of meat in a skillet just until done.

Transfer the cooked meat to a plate, and make a simple pan sauce by sautéing minced onions or shallots in the pan. Add a little Swanson® broth, Campbell's® French Onion Soup, wine or juice. Boil and stir constantly to scrape up all of the browned bits. Melt in a little butter. Serve the meat with the sauce. And don't forget sandwiches: Make them dinner-worthy with whole-grain or ethnic breads, and toast them on an indoor grill.

■ Get grilling: Speaking of grilling, it's a simple cooking method that seals in flavors in meats and brings out the sweetness of vegetables. Thinner cuts of meats and vegetables cook up fast on the grill, whether you use the outdoor or indoor variety.

■ No bones about it: Skinless, boneless chicken breasts are one of the most versatile meat cuts available today. They cook up fast and easy and can be used in dishes for almost every course.

■ Reconsider fish: Many home cooks find fish recipes intimidating, yet fish fillets are among the easiest of foods to prepare. Try this: Coat fillets in seasoned bread crumbs and lightly fry in a little olive or canola oil. In just a few minutes, you'll have a tender, delicious main dish that you can pair with about any vegetable and salad.

■ Don't forget your slow cooker: Toss in the ingredients in the morning, and dinner is ready when you get home in the evening.

■ Prep on weekends: Chop and refrigerate onions and other ingredients you plan to use during the week. Shred cheese and store in plastic bags in the fridge. Cook pasta and store in plastic lidded containers; to reheat, drop into boiling water just until hot. Grill, poach or fry up skinless, boneless chicken breasts; chop, and freeze in resealable bags to use during the week in soups, salads and casseroles. Cook ahead, and store in freezer or refrigerator.

■ Planned-overs: Cook more than you need so there will be ample leftovers for another meal. Then, plan a weekly leftover night and let everyone heat up what they want in the microwave.

Weeknight cooking doesn't just get food on the table; it also brings your family around the table. So get organized, get inspired and get cooking with Campbell's®.

Quick & Easy Fare

When time is not on your side, you can still get dinner on the table in 30 minutes or less

Chicken & Broccoli Alfredo

MAKES 4 SERVINGS

PREP
5 minutes

COOK
20 minutes

½ of a 16-ounce package linguine

1 cup fresh **or** frozen broccoli flowerets

2 tablespoons butter

1 pound skinless, boneless chicken breasts, cut into cubes

1 can (10¾ ounces) Campbell's® Condensed Cream of Mushroom Soup (Regular, 98% Fat Free **or** 25% Less Sodium)

½ cup milk

¼ teaspoon ground black pepper

½ cup grated Parmesan cheese

1. Prepare the linguine according to the package directions. Add the broccoli during the last 4 minutes of the cooking time. Drain the linguine and broccoli well in a colander and return them to the saucepot.

2. Heat the butter in a 10-inch skillet over medium-high heat. Add the chicken and cook for 10 minutes or until it's well browned, stirring often.

3. Stir the soup, milk, black pepper, cheese and linguine mixture into the skillet. Cook and stir until the chicken is cooked through. Serve with additional cheese.

Chicken Dijon with Noodles

PREP
5 minutes

COOK
25 minutes

2 tablespoons butter

4 skinless, boneless chicken breast halves

1 medium onion, chopped (about ½ cup)

1 can (10¾ ounces) Campbell's® Condensed Cream of Mushroom Soup (Regular, 98% Fat Free **or** 25% Less Sodium)

¼ cup apple juice **or** milk

1 tablespoon Dijon-style mustard

1 tablespoon chopped fresh parsley **or** 1 teaspoon dried parsley flakes

Hot cooked noodles

1. Heat the butter in a 10-inch skillet over medium-high heat. Add the chicken and cook for 10 minutes or until it's well browned on both sides. Remove the chicken and set aside.

2. Reduce the heat to medium. Add the onion and cook until tender.

3. Stir the soup, apple juice, mustard and parsley into the skillet. Heat to a boil. Return the chicken to the skillet and reduce the heat to low. Cover and cook for 5 minutes or until the chicken is cooked through. Serve with the noodles.

Lemony Olive Chicken

PREP
10 minutes

COOK
15 minutes

1 tablespoon vegetable oil

4 skinless, boneless chicken breast halves

1 can (10¾ ounces) Campbell's® Condensed Cream of Chicken Soup (Regular **or** 98% Fat Free)

¼ cup milk

1 tablespoon lemon juice

⅛ teaspoon ground black pepper

½ cup sliced pimento-stuffed Spanish olives

4 lemon slices

Hot cooked rice

1. Heat the oil in a 10-inch skillet over medium-high heat. Add the chicken and cook for 10 minutes or until it's well browned on both sides. Remove the chicken and set aside.

2. Stir the soup, milk, lemon juice, black pepper and olives into the skillet. Top with the lemon slices. Heat to a boil. Return the chicken to the skillet and reduce the heat to low. Cover and cook for 5 minutes or until the chicken is cooked through. Serve with the rice.

Citrus Balsamic Salmon

PREP
5 minutes

BAKE/COOK
20 minutes

8   fresh salmon fillets, ¾-inch thick (about 1½ pounds)
    Freshly ground black pepper
3   tablespoons olive oil
4½ teaspoons cornstarch
1¾ cups Swanson® Chicken Broth (Regular, Natural Goodness™
    or Certified Organic)
3   tablespoons balsamic vinegar
1   tablespoon orange juice
1   tablespoon brown sugar
1   teaspoon grated orange peel
    Orange slices for garnish, optional

1. Place the salmon in a 12×8×2-inch shallow baking dish. Sprinkle with the black pepper and drizzle with the oil. Bake at 350°F. for 15 minutes or until the fish flakes easily when tested with a fork.

2. Stir the cornstarch, broth, vinegar, orange juice, brown sugar and orange peel into a 2-quart saucepan over high heat. Cook and stir until the mixture boils and thickens.

3. Place the salmon on a serving platter and serve with the sauce. Garnish with the orange slices, if desired.

Garlic Pork Chops

PREP
 5 minutes

COOK
 20 minutes

1 tablespoon vegetable oil

4 boneless pork chops, ¾-inch thick (about 1 pound)

1 clove garlic, minced

1 can (10¾ ounces) Campbell's® Condensed Cream of Mushroom Soup (Regular, 98% Fat Free **or** 25% Less Sodium)

½ cup milk

4 cups hot cooked couscous **or** rice

1. Heat the oil in a 10-inch skillet over medium-high heat. Add the pork chops and garlic and cook for 10 minutes or until the chops are well browned on both sides. Remove the pork chops and set aside.

2. Stir the soup and milk into the skillet. Heat to a boil. Return the pork chops to the skillet and reduce the heat to low. Cover and cook for 5 minutes or until the chops are cooked through. Serve with the couscous or rice.

Penne with Creamy Vodka Sauce

PREP
5 minutes

COOK
20 minutes

2 jars (1 pound 10 ounces **each**) Prego® Chunky Garden
   Tomato, Onion & Garlic Italian Sauce

¼ cup vodka

⅓ cup chopped fresh basil leaves, optional

¼ teaspoon crushed red pepper

½ cup heavy cream

1 package (16 ounces) tube-shaped pasta (penne), cooked and
   drained

   Grated Parmesan cheese

1. Heat the Italian sauce, vodka, basil, if desired and red pepper in
a 3-quart saucepan over medium heat to a boil, stirring often. Remove
from the heat and stir in the cream.

2. Place the pasta in a large serving bowl. Pour the sauce mixture
over the pasta. Toss to coat. Sprinkle with the cheese.

Simple Salisbury Steak

PREP
5 minutes

COOK
25 minutes

1 pound ground beef

1 can (10¾ ounces) Campbell's® Condensed Cream of Mushroom Soup (Regular, 98% Fat Free **or** 25% Less Sodium)

⅓ cup dry bread crumbs

1 egg, beaten

1 small onion, finely chopped (about ¼ cup)

1 tablespoon vegetable oil

1½ cups sliced mushrooms

1. Thoroughly mix the beef, ¼ **cup** of the soup, bread crumbs, egg and onion in a medium bowl. Shape the mixture into 4 (½-inch-thick) burgers.

2. Heat the oil in a 10-inch skillet over medium-high heat. Add the burgers and cook until well browned on both sides. Remove the burgers with a slotted spatula and set aside.

3. Stir the remaining soup and mushrooms into the skillet. Heat to a boil. Return the burgers to the skillet and reduce the heat to low. Cover and cook for 10 minutes or until the burgers are cooked through.

Beef Taco Skillet

PREP
5 minutes

COOK
20 minutes

1 pound ground beef

1 can (10¾ ounces) Campbell's® Condensed Tomato Soup

1 cup Pace® Chunky Salsa **or** Picante Sauce

½ cup water

8 corn **or** flour tortillas (6-inch), cut into 1-inch pieces

1 cup shredded Cheddar cheese (4 ounces)

1. Cook the beef in a 10-inch skillet over medium-high heat until the beef is well browned, stirring frequently to break up meat. Pour off any fat.

2. Stir the soup, salsa, water, tortillas and **half** the cheese into the skillet. Heat to a boil. Reduce the heat to low. Cover and cook for 5 minutes or until hot and bubbling.

3. Top with the remaining cheese.

Autumn Pork Chops

PREP
5 minutes

COOK
20 minutes

1 tablespoon vegetable oil

4 bone-in pork chops, ½-inch thick

1 can (10¾ ounces) Campbell's® Condensed Cream of Celery Soup (Regular **or** 98% Fat Free)

½ cup apple juice **or** water

2 tablespoons spicy-brown mustard

1 tablespoon honey

Generous dash ground black pepper

Hot cooked medium egg noodles

1. Heat the oil in a 10-inch skillet over medium-high heat. Add the pork chops and cook until the chops are well browned on both sides. Remove the pork chops and set aside.

2. Stir the soup, apple juice, mustard, honey and black pepper into the skillet. Heat to a boil. Return the pork chops to the skillet and reduce the heat to low. Cover and cook for 5 minutes or until the chops are cooked through. Serve with the noodles.

Cranberry Chicken

1 tablespoon vegetable oil

4 skinless, boneless chicken breast halves

1 can (10¾ ounces) Campbell's® Condensed Cream of Mushroom Soup (Regular, 98% Fat Free **or** 25% Less Sodium)

¼ cup cranberry juice

¼ cup orange juice

1 tablespoon dried cranberries

1 tablespoon chopped fresh sage leaves **or** 1 teaspoon dried sage leaves, crushed

⅛ teaspoon ground black pepper

Hot cooked rice

Sliced green onions, optional

PREP
5 minutes

COOK
20 minutes

1. Heat the oil in a 10-inch skillet over medium-high heat. Add the chicken and cook for 10 minutes or until it's well browned on both sides. Remove the chicken and set aside.

2. Stir in the soup, cranberry juice, orange juice, cranberries, sage and black pepper. Heat to a boil. Return the chicken to the skillet and reduce the heat to low. Cover and cook for 5 minutes or until the chicken is cooked through.

3. Serve with the rice and sprinkle with the green onions, if desired.

Chicken Quesadillas & Fiesta Rice

PREP
10 minutes

BAKE
5 minutes

1   can (10¾ ounces) Campbell's® Condensed Cheddar
    Cheese Soup

¼   cup Pace® Picante Sauce

1½ cups chopped cooked chicken

8   flour tortillas (8-inch), warmed

Fiesta Rice

1. Heat the oven to 425°F.

2. Stir the soup, picante sauce and chicken in a medium bowl.

3. Place the tortillas on **2** baking sheets. Top **half** of each tortilla with ¼ **cup** of the soup mixture. Spread to within ½ inch of the edge. Moisten the edge of each tortilla with water. Fold over and press the edges together to seal.

4. Bake for 5 minutes or until the filling is hot.

Fiesta Rice: Heat 1 can (10½ ounces) Campbell's® Condensed **Chicken Broth**, ½ cup water and ½ cup Pace® **Chunky Salsa** in a 2-quart saucepan over medium-high heat to a boil. Stir in **2 cups uncooked instant white rice.** Cover the saucepan and remove from heat. Let stand 5 minutes. Fluff the rice with a fork.

Chicken Scampi

2 tablespoons butter

4 skinless, boneless chicken breast halves

1 can (10¾ ounces) Campbell's® Condensed Cream of Chicken Soup (Regular **or** 98% Fat Free)

¼ cup water

2 teaspoons lemon juice

2 cloves garlic, minced **or** ½ teaspoon garlic powder

   Hot cooked pasta

PREP
5 minutes

COOK
20 minutes

1. Heat the butter in a 10-inch skillet over medium-high heat. Add the chicken and cook for 10 minutes or until it's well browned on both sides. Remove the chicken and set aside.

2. Stir in the soup, water, lemon juice and garlic. Heat to a boil. Return the chicken to the skillet and reduce the heat to low. Cover and cook for 5 minutes or until chicken is cooked through.

3. Serve with the pasta.

Simply add a salad, and you have an entire

dinner with a minimum of fuss

Mushroom-Garlic Chicken

MAKES 4 SERVINGS

PREP
5 minutes

COOK
20 minutes

1 tablespoon vegetable oil

4 skinless, boneless chicken breast halves

1 can (10¾ ounces) Campbell's® Condensed Cream of Mushroom with Roasted Garlic Soup

½ cup milk

1. Heat the oil in a 10-inch skillet over medium-high heat. Add the chicken and cook for 10 minutes or until it's well browned on both sides. Remove the chicken from the skillet and set aside.

2. Stir the soup and milk into the skillet. Heat to a boil. Return the chicken to the skillet and reduce the heat to low. Cover and cook for 5 minutes or until the chicken is cooked through.

Zesty Chicken Mozzarella Sandwiches

PREP
10 minutes

MARINATE
10 minutes

BAKE
10 minutes

GRILL
15 minutes

⅓ cup prepared Italian salad dressing

4 skinless, boneless chicken breast halves

1 loaf (11.75 ounces) Pepperidge Farm® Frozen Mozzarella Garlic Cheese Bread

1 medium red onion, sliced (about ½ cup)

1. Pour the dressing in a shallow nonmetallic dish. Add the chicken and turn to coat. Cover and refrigerate for 10 minutes.

2. Heat the oven to 400°F. Remove the bread from the bag. Place the frozen bread halves, cut-side up, on an ungreased baking sheet. (If bread halves are frozen together, carefully insert a fork between the halves to separate.)

3. Place the baking sheet on the middle oven rack. Bake for 10 minutes or until heated through.

4. Remove the chicken from the marinade. Lightly oil the grill rack and heat the grill to medium-high. Grill the chicken for 15 minutes or until the chicken is cooked through, turning the chicken over halfway through cooking and brushing it often with the dressing. Throw away any remaining marinade.

5. Place the chicken and red onion on the bottom bread half. Top with the remaining bread half. Cut it into quarters.

Souper Filled Pastry Crust Bowls

THAW
40 minutes

PREP
5 minutes

BAKE
20 minutes

½ package (17.3 ounces) Pepperidge Farm® Frozen Puff Pastry Sheets (1 sheet)

1 egg

1 tablespoon water

Assorted fresh herb leaves (rosemary, thyme **or** sage), optional

1 can (18.6 to 19 ounces) Campbell's® Chunky™ Soup **or** Chili, any variety

---

EASY SUBSTITUTION TIP

Bake 1 package (10 ounces) Pepperidge Farm® Frozen Puff Pastry Shells according to the package directions. Heat the soup or chili according to the package directions. Place the shells on serving plates or bowls, push in the pastry centers and divide the soup among the shells.

---

1. Thaw the pastry sheet at room temperature for 40 minutes or until it's easy to handle. Heat the oven to 400°F. Stir the egg and water.

2. Unfold the pastry sheet on a lightly floured surface. Cut in half. Roll each half into a 9×9-inch square. Press pastry into **2** oven-safe bowls (16 ounces **each**), fold over the corners to make a rim. Press the herb leaves into the pastry, if desired. Brush lightly with the egg mixture.

3. Bake for 20 minutes or until golden. Let cool on a wire rack for 5 minutes.

4. Heat the soup or chili according to the package directions.

5. Remove the pastry from the bowls and place on 2 serving plates or bowls. Using a small knife, cut a slit into the center and push down to form a bowl. Divide the soup between the pastry bowls. Serve immediately.

French Onion Burgers

PREP
5 minutes

COOK
20 minutes

1 pound ground beef

1 can (10½ ounces) Campbell's® Condensed French Onion Soup

4 slices cheese

4 round hard rolls, split

1. Shape the beef into 4 (½-inch-thick) burgers.

2. Heat a 10-inch skillet over medium-high heat. Add the burgers and cook until they're well browned on both sides. Remove the burgers and set aside. Pour off any fat.

3. Stir the soup into the skillet. Heat to a boil. Return the burgers to the skillet and reduce the heat to low. Cover and cook for 5 minutes or until the burgers are cooked through. Top with cheese and continue cooking until the cheese melts. Serve burgers in rolls with soup mixture for dipping.

Pasta Primavera

3 cups **uncooked** corkscrew-shaped pasta (rotini)

1 bag (16 ounces) frozen vegetable combination (broccoli, cauliflower, carrots)

1 jar (1 pound 10 ounces) Prego® Traditional Italian Sauce

Grated Parmesan cheese

PREP
5 minutes

COOK
20 minutes

1. Prepare the pasta according to the package directions. Add the vegetables during the last 5 minutes of the cooking time. Drain the pasta and vegetables well in a colander.

2. Heat the sauce in the same saucepot over medium heat to a boil. Stir in the pasta and vegetables. Toss to coat. Top with the cheese.

Sirloin Steak Picante

PREP
5 minutes

GRILL
22 minutes

STAND
10 minutes

1½   pounds boneless beef sirloin **or** top round steak, 1½ inches thick

1   jar (16 ounces) Pace® Picante Sauce **or** Chunky Salsa

1. Lightly oil the grill rack and heat the grill to medium. Grill the steak for 22 minutes for medium-rare or to desired doneness, turning the steak over halfway through cooking and brushing often with **1 cup** of the picante sauce.

2. Let stand for 10 minutes before slicing.

3. Serve additional picante sauce with the steak.

Nacho Pasta

MAKES 4 SERVINGS

PREP
15 minutes

COOK
5 minutes

1   can (11 ounces) Campbell's® Condensed Fiesta Nacho Cheese Soup

½   cup milk

4   cups corkscrew-shaped pasta (rotini), cooked and drained

1. Heat the soup and milk in a 2-quart saucepan over medium heat. Cook and stir until hot and bubbling.

2. Stir in the pasta. Cook and stir until hot.

Sirloin Steak Picante

Creamy Chicken & Pasta

PREP
5 minutes

COOK
20 minutes

2　tablespoons vegetable oil

2　pounds skinless, boneless chicken breasts, cut into cubes

1　can (26 ounces) Campbell's® Condensed Cream of Chicken Soup

1　cup water

2　bags (16 ounces **each**) frozen vegetable and pasta blend

1. Heat the oil in a 12-inch skillet over medium-high heat. Add the chicken and cook until it's well browned, stirring often.

2. Stir the soup, water and vegetable pasta blend into the skillet. Heat to a boil. Reduce the heat to low. Cover and cook for 5 minutes or until the chicken and pasta are done.

Inside-Out Chicken Pot Pie

1 pound skinless, boneless chicken breasts, cut into cubes

1 can (10¾ ounces) Campbell's® Condensed Cream of Chicken Soup (Regular **or** 98% Fat Free)

1 bag (16 ounces) frozen vegetable combination (broccoli, cauliflower, carrots)

8 hot biscuits, split

PREP
5 minutes

COOK
20 minutes

1. Cook the chicken in a 10-inch nonstick skillet over medium-high heat until it's well browned, stirring often.

2. Stir the soup and vegetables into the skillet. Heat to a boil. Reduce the heat to low. Cover and cook for 5 minutes or until the chicken is cooked through.

3. Divide the chicken mixture among the biscuits.

Tasty Pork Chops

PREP
5 minutes

COOK
20 minutes

1 tablespoon vegetable oil

4 pork chops, (about 1 pound), ½-inch thick

1 can (10¾ ounces) Campbell's® Condensed Cream of Mushroom Soup (Regular, 98% Fat Free **or** 25% Less Sodium)

½ cup water

1. Heat the oil in a 10-inch skillet over medium-high heat. Add the chops and cook for 10 minutes or until browned on both sides. Remove the chops and set aside.

2. Stir the soup and water into the skillet. Heat to a boil. Return the chops to the skillet and reduce the heat to low. Cover and cook for 5 minutes or until the chops are cooked through.

Simply Delicious Meat Loaf & Gravy

1½ pounds ground beef

½ cup Italian-seasoned dry bread crumbs

1 egg, beaten

1 can (10¾ ounces) Campbell's® Condensed Golden
Mushroom Soup

¼ cup water

PREP
5 minutes

BAKE
1 hour

STAND
10 minutes

1. Thoroughly mix the beef, bread crumbs and egg in a large bowl.
Put the mixture into a 13×9×2-inch baking pan and firmly shape into
an 8×4-inch loaf.

2. Bake at 350°F. for 30 minutes. Spread ½ **can** of the soup over the
top of the meat loaf. Bake for 30 minutes more or until meat loaf is
cooked through. Remove the meat loaf from the pan to a cutting board
and let it stand for 10 minutes before slicing.

3. Heat **2 tablespoons** of the pan drippings, remaining soup and water
in a 1-quart saucepan over medium-high heat to a boil. Serve with the
meat loaf.

Skillet Chicken Parmesan

PREP
5 minutes

COOK
25 minutes

STAND
5 minutes

6   tablespoons grated Parmesan cheese

1½ cups Prego® Traditional Italian Sauce **or** Prego® Organic
Tomato & Basil Italian Sauce

Vegetable cooking spray

6   skinless, boneless chicken breast halves

1½ cups shredded part-skim mozzarella cheese (6 ounces)

1. Stir **4 tablespoons** of the Parmesan cheese into the sauce.

2. Spray a 12-inch skillet with cooking spray and heat over medium-high
heat for 1 minute. Add the chicken and cook for 10 minutes or until
it's well browned on both sides.

3. Pour the sauce mixture over the chicken, turning to coat with sauce.
Reduce the heat to medium. Cover and cook for 5 minutes or until
chicken is cooked through.

4. Top with the mozzarella cheese and remaining Parmesan cheese.
Let stand for 5 minutes or until the cheese melts.

Souper Sloppy Joes

1   pound ground beef

1   can (10¾ ounces) Campbell's® Condensed Tomato Soup
    (Regular **or** Healthy Request®)

¼   cup water

1   tablespoon prepared yellow mustard

6   hamburger rolls, split

PREP
5 minutes

COOK
15 minutes

1. Cook the beef in a 10-inch skillet over medium-high heat until the beef is well browned, stirring frequently to break up meat. Pour off any fat.

2. Stir the soup, water and mustard into the skillet. Cook and stir until the mixture is hot and bubbling.

3. Divide the beef mixture among the rolls.

Break out the slow cooker, and have dinner

ready and waiting when you get home

Chicken Cacciatore

MAKES 6 SERVINGS

PREP
10 minutes

COOK
7 to 8 hours
10 minutes

1¾ cups Swanson® Chicken Broth (Regular, Natural Goodness™ **or** Certified Organic)

1 teaspoon garlic powder

2 cans (14½ ounces **each**) diced Italian-style tomatoes

4 cups mushrooms cut in half (about 12 ounces)

2 large onions, chopped (about 2 cups)

3 pounds chicken parts, skin removed

Hot cooked spaghetti

1. Stir the broth, garlic powder, tomatoes, mushrooms and onions in a 3½-quart slow cooker. Add the chicken and turn to coat with the broth mixture.

2. Cover and cook on LOW for 7 to 8 hours* or until the chicken is cooked through. Serve over the spaghetti.

Or on HIGH for 4 to 5 hours

For thicker sauce, stir **2 tablespoons cornstarch** and **2 tablespoons water** in a small cup. Remove the chicken from the cooker. Stir the cornstarch mixture into the cooker. Turn heat to HIGH. Cover and cook for 10 minutes or until the mixture boils and thickens.

Swiss Steak

PREP
15 minutes

COOK
8 to 10 hours

1½ pounds boneless beef round steak, cut into 6 pieces

6 to 8 new potatoes (about ½ pound), cut into quarters

1½ cups fresh **or** frozen whole baby carrots

1 medium onion, sliced (about ½ cup)

1 can (14½ ounces) diced tomatoes with basil, garlic and oregano

1 can (10¼ ounces) Campbell's® Beef Gravy

1. Cook the beef in 2 batches in a 12-inch nonstick skillet over medium-high heat until it's well browned on all sides, stirring often.

2. Place the beef, potatoes, carrots and onion in a 3½-quart slow cooker. Stir the tomatoes and gravy. Pour over beef and vegetables.

3. Cover and cook on LOW for 8 to 10 hours* or until the beef is fork-tender.

Or on HIGH for 4 to 5 hours

Nacho Chicken & Rice Wraps

PREP
10 minutes

COOK
7 to 8 hours

2 cans (10¾ ounces **each**) Campbell's® Condensed Cheddar Cheese Soup

2 cups Pace® Chunky Salsa **or** Picante Sauce

1 cup water

1¼ cups **uncooked** regular long-grain white rice

2 pounds skinless, boneless chicken breasts, cut into cubes

10 flour tortillas (10-inch), warmed

EASY SUBSTITUTION TIP

For a firmer rice, substitute converted rice for regular.

1. Stir the soup, salsa, water, rice and chicken in a 3½-quart slow cooker.

2. Cover and cook on LOW for 7 to 8 hours* or until chicken is cooked through.

3. Spoon about **1 cup** rice mixture down the center of each tortilla. Fold tortilla around filling.

Or on HIGH for 4 to 5 hours

Swiss Steak

Veal Stew with Garden Vegetables

PREP
15 minutes

COOK
8 to 10 hours

EASY SUBSTITUTION TIP

Substitute skinless, boneless chicken thighs, cut into 1-inch pieces for the veal.

2 to 2½ pounds veal for stew, cut into 1-inch pieces

Ground black pepper

2 tablespoons olive oil

1 bag (16 ounces) fresh **or** frozen whole baby carrots (about 2½ cups)

1 large onion, diced (about 1 cup)

4 cloves garlic, minced

¼ cup all-purpose flour

2 cups Swanson® Chicken Broth (Regular, Natural Goodness™ **or** Certified Organic)

½ teaspoon dried rosemary leaves, crushed

1 can (14½ ounces) diced tomatoes

1 cup frozen peas

Hot cooked rice **or** barley

1. Season the veal with the black pepper.

2. Heat the oil in a 6-quart saucepot. Add the veal in 2 batches and cook until it's well browned, stirring often. Remove the veal with a slotted spoon and put it in a 3½- to 6-quart slow cooker.

3. Add the carrots, onion and garlic. Sprinkle with the flour and toss to coat. Stir the broth, rosemary and tomatoes into the cooker.

4. Cover and cook on LOW for 7 to 8 hours*.

5. Stir the peas into the cooker. Cover and cook for 1 hour more or until the meat is fork-tender. Serve over the rice or barley.

Or on HIGH for 4 to 5 hours

Chicken Rice Soup

PREP
15 minutes

COOK
7 to 8 hours

½ cup **uncooked** wild rice

½ cup **uncooked** regular long-grain white rice

1 tablespoon vegetable oil

5¼ cups Swanson® Chicken Broth (Regular, Natural Goodness™ **or** Certified Organic)

2 teaspoons dried thyme leaves, crushed

¼ teaspoon crushed red pepper

2 stalks celery, coarsely chopped (about 1 cup)

1 medium onion, chopped (about ½ cup)

1 pound skinless, boneless chicken breasts, cut into cubes

Sour cream

Chopped green onions

1. Stir the wild rice, white rice and oil in a 3½-quart slow cooker. Cover and cook on HIGH for 15 minutes.

2. Stir the broth, thyme, red pepper, celery, onion and chicken into the cooker. Turn the heat to LOW. Cover and cook on LOW for 7 to 8 hours* or until the chicken is cooked through.

3. Serve with the sour cream and green onions.

*Or on HIGH for 4 to 5 hours

Creamy Blush Sauce with Turkey and Penne

MAKES 8 SERVINGS

4   turkey thighs, skin removed (about 3 pounds)

1   jar (1 pound 9.75 ounces) Prego® Chunky Garden Mushroom & Green Pepper Italian Sauce

½   teaspoon crushed red pepper

½   cup half-and-half

   Tube-shaped pasta (penne), cooked and drained

   Grated Parmesan cheese

PREP
10 minutes

COOK
7 to 8 hours

1. Put the turkey in a 3½- to 5-quart slow cooker. Pour the Italian sauce over the turkey and sprinkle with the red pepper.

2. Cover and cook on LOW for 7 to 8 hours* or until the turkey is fork-tender and cooked through. Remove the turkey from the cooker. Remove the turkey meat from the bones.

3. Stir the turkey meat and the half-and-half into the cooker. Cover and cook for 10 minutes or until hot. Spoon the sauce over the turkey and pasta. Sprinkle with the cheese.

Or on HIGH for 4 to 5 hours

EASY SUBSTITUTION TIP

Substitute 8 bone-in chicken thighs (about 2 pounds) for the turkey thighs. Makes 4 servings.

Autumn Brisket

PREP
20 minutes

COOK
8 to 9 hours

3-pound boneless beef brisket

1 small head cabbage (about 1 pound), cut into 8 wedges

1 large sweet potato (about ¾ pound), peeled and cut into 1-inch pieces

1 large onion, cut into 8 wedges

1 medium Granny Smith apple, cored and cut into 8 wedges

2 cans (10¾ ounces **each**) Campbell's® Condensed Cream of Celery Soup (Regular **or** 98% Fat Free)

1 cup water

2 teaspoons caraway seed, optional

1. Season brisket, if desired.

2. Put the brisket in a 6-quart slow cooker. Top with the cabbage, sweet potato, onion and apple.

3. Stir the soup, water and caraway, if desired in a medium bowl. Pour the soup mixture over the brisket and vegetable mixture.

4. Cover and cook on LOW for 8 to 9 hours* or until the meat is fork-tender.

5. Remove the brisket from the cooker to a cutting board and let it stand for 10 minutes. Thinly slice brisket across the grain. Arrange brisket on a serving platter. Remove the vegetables and fruit with a slotted spoon and put on platter. Pour the pan juices into a gravy boat and serve with the brisket.

*Or on HIGH for 4 to 5 hours

Barley and Lentil Soup

8 cups Swanson® Beef Broth (Regular, Lower Sodium **or** Certified Organic)

2 cloves garlic, minced

1 teaspoon dried oregano leaves, crushed

4 large carrots, sliced (about 3 cups)

1 large onion, chopped (about 1 cup)

½ cup **uncooked** barley

½ cup dried lentils

PREP
10 minutes

COOK
8 to 9 hours

1. Stir the broth, garlic, oregano, carrots, onion, barley and lentils in a 3½- to 6-quart slow cooker.

2. Cover and cook on LOW for 8 to 9 hours* or until the barley and lentils are tender.

Or on HIGH for 4 to 5 hours

Chipotle Chili

PREP
15 minutes

COOK
8 to 9 hours

EASY SUBSTITUTION TIP

Use your favorite shredded cheese for the Cheddar.

1 jar (16 ounces) Pace® Chipotle Chunky Salsa

1 cup water

2 tablespoons chili powder

1 large onion, chopped (about 1 cup)

2 pounds beef for stew, cut into ½-inch pieces

1 can (about 19 ounces) red kidney beans, rinsed and drained

Shredded Cheddar cheese, optional

Sour cream, optional

1. Stir the salsa, water, chili powder, onion, beef and beans in a 3½-quart slow cooker.

2. Cover and cook on LOW for 8 to 9 hours* or until the meat is fork-tender. Serve with the cheese and sour cream, if desired.

Or on HIGH for 4 to 5 hours

Chicken in Creamy Sun-Dried Tomato Sauce

MAKES 8 SERVINGS

2 cans (10¾ ounces **each**) Campbell's® Condensed Cream of Chicken Soup with Herbs

1 cup Chablis **or** other dry white wine

¼ cup coarsely chopped pitted kalamata **or** oil-cured olives

2 tablespoons drained capers

2 cloves garlic, minced

1 can (14 ounces) artichoke hearts, drained and chopped

1 cup drained, coarsely chopped sun-dried tomatoes

8 skinless, boneless chicken breast halves

½ cup chopped fresh basil leaves, optional

Hot cooked rice, egg noodles **or** seasoned mashed potatoes

PREP
15 minutes

COOK
7 to 8 hours

EASY SUBSTITUTION TIP

*Substitute Swanson®
Chicken Broth
(Regular, Natural
Goodness™ **or**
Certified Organic)
for the wine.*

1. Stir the soup, wine, olives, capers, garlic, artichokes and tomatoes in a 3½-quart slow cooker. Add the chicken and turn to coat with the soup mixture.

2. Cover and cook on LOW for 7 to 8 hours* or until chicken is cooked through. Sprinkle with basil, if desired. Serve with rice, noodles or potatoes.

Or on HIGH for 4 to 5 hours

Ratatouille with Penne

PREP
15 minutes

COOK
5½ to 6 hours

1 can (10¾ ounces) Campbell's® Condensed Tomato Soup

1 tablespoon olive oil

⅛ teaspoon ground black pepper

1 small eggplant, peeled and cut into ½-inch cubes (about 5 cups)

1 medium zucchini, thinly sliced (about 1½ cups)

1 medium red pepper, diced (about 1 cup)

1 large onion, sliced (about 1 cup)

1 clove garlic, minced

Tube-shaped pasta (penne), cooked and drained

Grated Parmesan cheese, optional

1. Stir the soup, olive oil, black pepper, eggplant, zucchini, red pepper, onion and garlic in a 4- to 5½-quart slow cooker.

2. Cover and cook on LOW for 5½ to 6 hours* or until the vegetables are tender.

3. Serve over the pasta. Serve with the cheese, if desired.

Or on HIGH for 2½ to 3 hours

Pulled Pork Sandwiches

MAKES 12 SANDWICHES

1	tablespoon vegetable oil
	3½- to 4-pound boneless pork shoulder roast, netted **or** tied
1	can (10½ ounces) Campbell's® Condensed French Onion Soup
1	cup ketchup
¼	cup cider vinegar
3	tablespoons packed brown sugar
12	round sandwich rolls, split

PREP
15 minutes

COOK
8 to 10 hours

STAND
10 minutes

1. Heat the oil in a 10-inch skillet over medium-high heat. Add the roast and cook until it's well browned on all sides.

2. Stir the soup, ketchup, vinegar and brown sugar in a 5-quart slow cooker. Add the roast and turn to coat with the soup mixture.

3. Cover and cook on LOW for 8 to 10 hours* or until the meat is fork-tender.

4. Remove the roast from the cooker to a cutting board and let it stand for 10 minutes. Using 2 forks, shred the pork. Return the shredded pork to the cooker.

5. Divide the pork and sauce mixture among the rolls.

Or on HIGH for 4 to 5 hours

Hearty Mixed Bean Stew with Sausage

MAKES 8 SERVINGS

PREP
15 minutes

COOK
8 to 9 hours

¾ pound sweet Italian pork sausage, casing removed

10 cups Swanson® Chicken Broth (Regular, Natural Goodness™ **or** Certified Organic)

¼ teaspoon ground black pepper

2 medium carrots, chopped (about ⅔ cup)

1 stalk celery, chopped (about ½ cup)

¾ cup **each** dried pinto, navy **and** kidney beans

6 sun-dried tomatoes in oil, drained and thinly sliced (about ¼ cup)

Grated Parmesan cheese

1. Cook the sausage in a 10-inch skillet over medium-high heat until sausage is well browned, stirring frequently to break up meat. Remove the sausage with a slotted spoon and put in a 5- to 5½-quart slow cooker.

2. Stir the broth, black pepper, carrots, celery and pinto, navy and kidney beans into the cooker.

3. Cover and cook on LOW for 7 or 8 hours*.

4. Stir in the tomatoes. Cover and cook for 1 hour more or until the beans are tender. Serve with the cheese.

*Or on HIGH for 4 to 4½ hours

Golden Mushroom Pork & Apples

MAKES 8 SERVINGS

2   cans (10¾ ounces **each**) Campbell's® Condensed Golden Mushroom Soup

½   cup water

1   tablespoon packed brown sugar

1   tablespoon Worcestershire sauce

1   teaspoon dried thyme leaves, crushed

8   boneless pork chops, ¾-inch thick (about 2 pounds)

4   large Granny Smith apples, sliced (about 6 cups)

2   large onions, sliced (about 2 cups)

PREP
10 minutes

COOK
8 to 9 hours

1. Stir the soup, water, brown sugar, Worcestershire and thyme in a 3½-quart slow cooker. Add the pork and turn to coat with the soup mixture. Top with the apples and onions.

2. Cover and cook on LOW for 8 to 9 hours* or until the pork is cooked through.

*Or on HIGH for 4 to 5 hours

Casserole Favorites

The mainstay of American weeknight menus

is still one of the simplest and most satisfying

Baked Pork Chops with Garden Stuffing

MAKES 6 SERVINGS

PREP
10 minutes

BAKE
40 minutes

Vegetable cooking spray

1   can (10¾ ounces) Campbell's® Condensed Golden Mushroom Soup

¾   cup water

1   bag (16 ounces) frozen vegetable combination (broccoli, cauliflower, carrots)

1   tablespoon butter

4   cups Pepperidge Farm® Herb Seasoned Stuffing

6   boneless pork chops, ¾-inch thick

1. Spray a 13×9×2-inch shallow baking dish with cooking spray.

2. Stir ⅓ **cup** of the soup, ½ **cup** of the water, vegetables and butter in a 2-quart saucepan. Heat to a boil. Remove from the heat. Add the stuffing and stir lightly to coat.

3. Spoon the stuffing mixture into the prepared dish. Arrange the chops over the stuffing mixture.

4. Stir the remaining soup and remaining water. Spoon over the chops.

5. Bake at 400°F. for 40 minutes or until the chops are cooked through.

Cornbread Chicken Pot Pie

PREP
10 minutes

BAKE
15 minutes

1 can (10¾ ounces) Campbell's® Condensed Cream of Chicken Soup (Regular **or** 98% Fat Free)

⅛ teaspoon ground black pepper

2 cups cubed cooked chicken

1 can (about 8 ounces) whole kernel corn, drained

1 package (11 ounces) refrigerated cornbread twists

1. Heat the oven to 425°F.

2. Stir the soup, black pepper, chicken and corn in a 2-quart saucepan over medium heat. Cook and stir until hot and bubbling. Pour the chicken mixture into a 9-inch pie plate.

3. Separate the cornbread into **8** pieces along the perforations. (Do not unroll the dough.) Place over the hot chicken mixture.

4. Bake for 15 minutes or until the cornbread is golden.

Sloppy Joe Casserole

PREP
  10 minutes

BAKE
  15 minutes

1 pound ground beef

1 can (10¾ ounces) Campbell's® Condensed Tomato Soup

¼ cup water

1 teaspoon Worcestershire sauce

⅛ teaspoon ground black pepper

1 package (7.5 ounces) refrigerated biscuits (10)

½ cup shredded Cheddar cheese

1. Heat the oven to 400°F.

2. Cook the beef in a 10-inch skillet over medium-high heat until the beef is well browned, stirring frequently to break up meat. Pour off any fat.

3. Stir the soup, water, Worcestershire and black pepper into the skillet. Heat to a boil. Spoon the beef mixture into a 1½-quart casserole. Arrange the biscuits over the beef mixture around the edge of the casserole.

4. Bake for 15 minutes or until the biscuits are golden brown. Sprinkle the cheese over the beef mixture.

Ham Asparagus Gratin

PREP
20 minutes

BAKE
30 minutes

1 can (10¾ ounces) Campbell's® Condensed Cream of Asparagus Soup

½ cup milk

¼ teaspoon onion powder

⅛ teaspoon ground black pepper

1½ cups cooked cut asparagus

1½ cups cubed cooked ham

2¼ cups corkscrew-shaped pasta (rotini), cooked and drained

1 cup shredded Cheddar **or** Swiss cheese (4 ounces)

1. Stir the soup, milk, onion powder, black pepper, asparagus, ham, pasta and ½ **cup** of the cheese in a 12×8×2-inch shallow baking dish.

2. Bake at 400°F. for 25 minutes or until hot. Stir.

3. Sprinkle with the remaining cheese. Bake 5 minutes more or until cheese melts.

Hearty Sausage & Rice Casserole

PREP
15 minutes

BAKE
1 hour

EASY SUBSTITUTION TIP

For an extra-special touch, substitute 1 package (8 ounces) baby portobello mushrooms, sliced, for the sliced mushrooms.

1	pound bulk pork sausage
1	package (8 ounces) sliced mushrooms (about 3 cups)
2	stalks celery, coarsely chopped (about 1 cup)
1	large red pepper, coarsely chopped (about 1 cup)
1	large onion, coarsely chopped (about 1 cup)
1	teaspoon dried thyme leaves, crushed
½	teaspoon dried marjoram leaves, crushed
1¾	cups Swanson® Chicken Broth (Regular, Natural Goodness™ **or** Certified Organic)
1	can (10¾ ounces) Campbell's® Condensed Cream of Mushroom Soup (Regular, 98% Fat Free **or** 25% Less Sodium)
1	box (6 ounces) long-grain and wild rice mix
1	cup shredded Cheddar cheese (4 ounces)

1. Cook the sausage in a 12-inch skillet over medium-high heat until the sausage is well browned, stirring frequently to break up meat. Pour off any fat.

2. Add the mushrooms, celery, pepper, onion, thyme, marjoram and seasoning packet from the rice blend and cook until the vegetables are tender-crisp.

3. Stir the broth, soup, rice blend and ½ **cup** of the cheese in a 13×9×2-inch shallow baking dish. Stir in the sausage mixture. **Cover.**

4. Bake at 375°F. for 1 hour or until the casserole is hot and bubbly and the rice is tender. Stir the rice mixture. Sprinkle with the remaining cheese.

Campbell's Kitchen Tip: To protect skillet handle, cover with foil.

Cheesy Chicken & Rice Casserole

PREP
5 minutes

BAKE
45 minutes

1 can (10¾ ounces) Campbell's® Condensed Cream of Chicken Soup (Regular **or** 98% Fat Free)

1⅓ cups water

¾ cup **uncooked** long-grain white rice

2 cups fresh **or** frozen vegetables

½ teaspoon onion powder

4 skinless, boneless chicken breast halves

½ cup shredded Cheddar cheese

1. Stir the soup, water, rice, vegetables and onion powder in a 12×8×2-inch shallow baking dish.

2. Top with the chicken. Season the chicken as desired. **Cover**.

3. Bake at 375°F. for 45 minutes or until chicken is cooked through. Top with the cheese.

Tuna Noodle Casserole

2   cans (10¾ ounces **each**) Campbell's® Condensed Cream of
    Mushroom Soup (Regular, 98% Fat Free **or** 25% Less Sodium)

¾   cup milk

1½ cups cooked peas

3   cans (about 6 ounces **each**) tuna, drained and flaked

3   cups hot cooked medium egg noodles

¾   cup shredded Cheddar cheese

PREP
10 minutes

BAKE
25 minutes

1. Stir the soup, milk, peas, tuna and noodles in a 2-quart casserole.

2. Bake at 400°F. for 25 minutes or until hot. Stir.

3. Sprinkle cheese over the tuna mixture. Bake for 2 minutes more or until
the cheese melts.

Three Cheese Baked Ziti with Spinach

PREP
15 minutes

BAKE
30 minutes

1 package (16 ounces) medium tube-shaped pasta (ziti)

1 bag (6 ounces) baby spinach leaves (4 cups), washed

1 jar (1 pound 9 ounces) Prego® Marinara Italian Sauce

1 cup ricotta cheese

1 cup shredded mozzarella cheese (4 ounces)

¾ cup grated Parmesan cheese

½ teaspoon garlic powder

¼ teaspoon ground black pepper

1. Prepare the pasta according to the package directions. Add the spinach during the last minute of the cooking time. Drain the pasta and spinach well in a colander. Return them to the saucepot.

2. Stir the Italian sauce, ricotta, ½ **cup** of the mozzarella cheese, ½ **cup** of the Parmesan cheese, garlic powder and black pepper into the pasta mixture. Spoon the pasta mixture into a 13×9×2-inch shallow baking dish. Sprinkle with the remaining mozzarella and Parmesan cheeses.

3. Bake at 350°F. for 30 minutes or until hot and bubbly.

Enchilada-Style Casserole

2   cans (10¾ ounces **each**) Campbell's® Condensed Cheddar
    Cheese Soup

½   cup water

1   jar (16 ounces) Pace® Chunky Salsa

4   cups cubed cooked chicken

8   flour **or** 12 corn tortillas (6- to 8-inch), cut into strips

1   cup shredded Cheddar cheese (4 ounces)

PREP
10 minutes

BAKE
35 minutes

1. Stir the soup, water, ½ **cup** of the salsa and chicken in a large bowl.
Stir in the tortillas. Spread the chicken mixture in a 13×9×2-inch shallow
baking dish. Top with the cheese. **Cover.**

2. Bake at 350°F. for 35 minutes or until hot and bubbly. Serve with the
remaining salsa.

Asian Chicken & Rice Bake

PREP
  5 minutes

BAKE
  45 minutes

¾ cup **uncooked** regular long-grain white rice

4 skinless, boneless chicken breast halves

1 can (10¾ ounces) Campbell's® Condensed Golden Mushroom Soup

¾ cup water

2 tablespoons soy sauce

2 tablespoons cider vinegar

2 tablespoons honey

1 teaspoon garlic powder

    Paprika

CAMPBELL'S® KITCHEN TIP

Add 2 cups frozen broccoli flowerets to the rice before baking. Serve with your favorite stir-fry vegetable blend.

---

1. Spread the rice in a 12×8×2-inch shallow baking dish. Top with the chicken.

2. Stir the soup, water, soy sauce, vinegar, honey and garlic powder in a small bowl. Pour over the chicken. Sprinkle with the paprika. **Cover.**

3. Bake at 375°F. for 45 minutes or until the chicken is cooked through.

Beef Taco Casserole

MAKES 4 SERVINGS

1   pound ground beef

1   can (10¾ ounces) Campbell's® Condensed Tomato Soup

1   cup Pace® Chunky Salsa **or** Picante Sauce

½   cup milk

½   cup **uncooked** instant white rice

½   cup slightly crushed tortilla chips

½   cup shredded Cheddar cheese

PREP
10 minutes

BAKE
25 minutes

1. Cook the beef in a 10-inch skillet over medium-high heat until the beef is well browned, stirring frequently to break up meat. Pour off any fat.

2. Stir the soup, salsa, milk and rice into the skillet. Spoon the beef mixture into a 1½-quart casserole. **Cover.**

3. Bake at 400°F. for 25 minutes or until hot. Stir.

4. Arrange the chips around the edge of the casserole. Sprinkle with the cheese.

Garlic Shrimp & Broccoli with Pasta

PREP
15 minutes

BAKE
30 minutes

1 package (21.7 ounces) Campbell's® Supper Bakes® Garlic Chicken with Pasta (includes seasoning, pasta, baking sauce and crumb topping)

2¼ cups hot water

2 tablespoons butter, cut up

2 cups fresh **or** frozen broccoli flowerets

1½ pounds fresh large shrimp, peeled and deveined

1. Heat the oven to 400°F.

2. Stir the seasoning, hot water, butter, pasta and broccoli in a 13×9×2-inch shallow baking dish. Top with the shrimp.

3. Pour the baking sauce over the shrimp and pasta mixture. **Cover**.

4. Bake for 20 minutes. Uncover and stir the pasta around the edge of the dish. Sprinkle the crumb topping over the shrimp. Bake uncovered, for 10 minutes more or until the shrimp turn pink and the pasta is tender. Stir the pasta before serving.

Chicken Broccoli Divan

4 cups fresh **or** frozen broccoli flowerets

4 skinless, boneless chicken breast halves

1 can (10¾ ounces) Campbell's® Condensed Cream of Chicken Soup (Regular **or** 98% Fat Free)

½ cup milk

½ cup shredded Cheddar cheese

2 tablespoons dry bread crumbs

1 tablespoon butter, melted

PREP
10 minutes

BAKE
30 minutes

1. Arrange the broccoli and chicken in a 12×8×2-inch shallow baking dish.

2. Stir the soup and milk in a small bowl and pour over the broccoli and chicken.

3. Sprinkle the cheese over the soup mixture. Mix the bread crumbs with the butter in a small bowl and sprinkle over the cheese.

4. Bake at 350°F. for 30 minutes or until the chicken is cooked through and the bread crumbs are browned.

Sides, Salads and More

Round out dinner with these simple and delicious salads, side dishes and more

Sausage & Apple Stuffing

MAKES 5 CUPS

PREP
5 minutes

COOK
10 minutes

1¾ cups Swanson® Chicken Broth (Regular, Natural Goodness™ **or** Certified Organic)

Generous dash ground black pepper

1 stalk celery, coarsely chopped (about ½ cup)

1 small onion, coarsely chopped (about ¼ cup)

½ medium red apple, chopped

½ medium green apple, chopped

½ pound bulk pork sausage, cooked and crumbled

2 cups Pepperidge Farm® Cubed Herb Seasoned Stuffing

2 cups Pepperidge Farm® Corn Bread Stuffing

1. Heat the broth, black pepper, celery, onion and apples in a 3-quart saucepan over medium-high heat to a boil. Reduce the heat to low. Cover and cook for 5 minutes or until the vegetables are tender.

2. Add the sausage and stuffing and stir lightly to coat.

For an Interesting Twist: Omit the apples. Add ½ **teaspoon chili powder**. Use ½ **pound smoked chorizo sausage**, casing removed and cut into ½-inch pieces for the pork sausage.

Savory Vegetable Stuffing Bake

PREP
20 minutes

BAKE
30 minutes

¼ pound bulk pork sausage

1 large onion, chopped (about 1 cup)

½ teaspoon dried thyme leaves, crushed

1 can (10¾ ounces) Campbell's® Condensed Cream of Celery Soup (Regular **or** 98% Fat Free)

1 can (about 8 ounces) stewed tomatoes

2 cups frozen vegetable combination (broccoli, corn, red pepper)

3 cups Pepperidge Farm® Herb Seasoned Stuffing

1. Cook the sausage, onion and thyme in a 10-inch skillet over medium-high heat until the sausage is well browned, stirring frequently to break up meat. Pour off any fat.

2. Stir the soup, tomatoes and vegetables into the skillet. Heat to a boil. Remove from the heat. Add the stuffing and stir lightly to coat. Spoon the mixture into an 8×8-inch baking dish.

3. Bake at 350°F. for 30 minutes or until hot.

SIDES, SALADS AND MORE 81

Mediterranean Chop Salad

PREP
25 minutes

1 package (12 ounces) romaine lettuce hearts, chopped

1 large seedless cucumber, peeled and chopped (about 1⅔ cups)

3 stalks celery, sliced **or** 1 cup sliced fennel (about 1½ cups)

1 cup chopped roasted red **or** yellow sweet peppers

½ cup chopped pitted ripe olives

1 box (6 ounces) Pepperidge Farm® Croutons, any variety

½ cup prepared balsamic vinaigrette dressing

Freshly ground black pepper

Parmesan cheese shavings

1. Mix the lettuce, cucumber, celery, red pepper, olives and croutons in a 4-quart serving bowl.

2. Pour the dressing over the vegetables, tossing until well coated.

3. Serve immediately with the black pepper and cheese.

Corn and Black-Eyed Pea Salad

PREP
15 minutes

CHILL
4 hours

1   bag (16 ounces) frozen whole kernel corn, thawed (about 3 cups)

1   can (about 16 ounces) black-eyed peas, rinsed and drained

1   large green pepper, chopped (about 1 cup)

½   cup chopped red onion

½   cup chopped fresh cilantro leaves, optional

1   jar (16 ounces) Pace® Chunky Salsa

MAKE AHEAD TIP

Prepare the salad as directed. Cover and refrigerate the salad overnight. Stir the salad before serving.

1. Stir the corn, peas, green pepper, red onion and cilantro, if desired in a medium bowl. Stir the salsa into the corn mixture until well coated.

2. Cover and refrigerate the salad for 4 hours.

3. Stir the salad before serving.

Cooking for a Crowd: Recipe may be doubled.

Asian Chicken Noodle Soup

PREP
5 minutes

COOK
20 minutes

3½ cups Swanson® Chicken Broth (Regular, Natural Goodness™ **or** Certified Organic)

1 teaspoon soy sauce

1 teaspoon ground ginger

Generous dash ground black pepper

½ red pepper, cut into 2-inch-long strips (about ¾ cup)

1 medium carrot, diagonally sliced (about ½ cup)

1 stalk celery, diagonally sliced (about ½ cup)

2 medium green onions, diagonally sliced (about ¼ cup)

1 clove garlic, minced

½ cup broken-up **uncooked** curly Asian noodles

1 cup shredded cooked chicken

1. Heat the broth, soy sauce, ginger, black pepper, red pepper, carrot, celery, green onions and garlic in a 2-quart saucepan over medium-high heat to a boil.

2. Stir in the noodles and chicken. Reduce the heat to medium. Cook for 10 minutes or until the noodles are tender.

For an Interesting Twist: Use **1 cup sliced bok choy** for the celery and **2 ounces uncooked cellophane noodles** for the curly Asian noodles. Reduce the cook time to 5 minutes.

Souper Rice

1	can (10½ ounces) Campbell's® Condensed Vegetable Soup
1½	soup cans water
1	cup **uncooked** regular long-grain white rice

PREP
5 minutes

COOK
25 minutes

1. Heat the soup and water in a 2-quart saucepan over medium-high heat to a boil.

2. Stir in the rice. Reduce the heat to low. Cover the saucepan and cook for 20 minutes or until the rice is tender. Fluff the rice with a fork.

Scalloped Potato-Onion Bake

MAKES 6 SERVINGS

PREP
10 minutes

BAKE
1 hour 15 minutes

1   can (10¾ ounces) Campbell's® Condensed Cream of Celery Soup (Regular **or** 98% Fat Free)

½   cup milk

Dash ground black pepper

4   medium potatoes (about 1¼ pounds), thinly sliced

1   small onion, thinly sliced (about ¼ cup)

1   tablespoon butter, cut into pieces

Paprika

1. Stir the soup, milk and black pepper with a whisk or fork in a small bowl. Layer **half** of the potatoes, **half** of the onion and **half** of the soup mixture in a 1½-quart casserole. Repeat the layers. Place the butter over the soup mixture. Sprinkle with the paprika. Cover the dish with foil.

2. Bake at 400°F. for 1 hour. Uncover and bake for 15 minutes more or until the potatoes are fork-tender.

Cheddar Broccoli Bake

MAKES 6 SERVINGS

1 can (10¾ ounces) Campbell's® Condensed Cheddar Cheese Soup

½ cup milk

   Dash ground black pepper

4 cups cooked broccoli cuts

1 can (2.8 ounces) French fried onions (1⅓ cups)

PREP
10 minutes

BAKE
30 minutes

1. Stir the soup, milk, black pepper, broccoli and ⅔ **cup** of the onions in a 1½-quart casserole. **Cover.**

2. Bake at 350°F. for 25 minutes or until hot. Uncover and stir the broccoli mixture.

3. Sprinkle the remaining onions over the broccoli mixture. Bake for 5 minutes more or until the onions are golden.

Creamy Vegetable Medley

PREP
5 minutes

COOK
20 minutes

1   can (10¾ ounces) Campbell's® Condensed Cream of Celery Soup (Regular **or** 98% Fat Free)

½   cup milk

2   cups broccoli flowerets

2   medium carrots, cut up (about 1 cup)

1   cup cauliflower flowerets

Heat the soup, milk, broccoli, carrots and cauliflower in a 3-quart saucepan over medium-high heat to a boil. Reduce the heat to low. Cover and cook for 15 minutes or until the vegetables are tender.

Ultra Creamy Mashed Potatoes

MAKES ABOUT 6 SERVINGS

3½ cups Swanson® Chicken Broth (Regular, Natural Goodness™ **or** Certified Organic)

5 large potatoes, cut into 1-inch pieces (about 7½ cups)

½ cup light cream

2 tablespoons butter

Generous dash ground black pepper

1. Heat the broth and potatoes in a 3-quart saucepan over medium-high heat to a boil.

2. Reduce the heat to medium. Cover and cook for 10 minutes or until the potatoes are tender. Drain, reserving the broth.

3. Mash the potatoes with ¼ **cup** of the broth, cream, butter and black pepper. Add additional broth, if needed, until desired consistency.

PREP
5 minutes

COOK
20 minutes

TIP

Ultimate Mashed Potatoes: Stir ½ *cup sour cream,* 3 *slices bacon, cooked and crumbled (reserve some for garnish), and* ¼ *cup chopped fresh chives into hot mashed potatoes. Sprinkle with remaining bacon.*

Saucy Asparagus

PREP
5 minutes

COOK
10 minutes

1   can (10¾ ounces) Campbell's® Condensed Cream of Asparagus Soup

⅓   cup milk **or** water

2   pounds asparagus, trimmed **or** 2 packages (about 10 ounces **each**) frozen asparagus spears, cooked and drained

Heat the soup and milk in a 1-quart saucepan over medium-high heat. Cook and stir until the mixture is hot and bubbling. Serve over the asparagus.

index

METRIC CONVERSION CHART

VOLUME MEASUREMENTS (dry)

1/8 teaspoon = 0.5 mL
1/4 teaspoon = 1 mL
1/2 teaspoon = 2 mL
3/4 teaspoon = 4 mL
1 teaspoon = 5 mL
1 tablespoon = 15 mL
2 tablespoons = 30 mL
1/4 cup = 60 mL
1/3 cup = 75 mL
1/2 cup = 125 mL
2/3 cup = 150 mL
3/4 cup = 175 mL
1 cup = 250 mL
2 cups = 1 pint = 500 mL
3 cups = 750 mL
4 cups = 1 quart = 1 L

VOLUME MEASUREMENTS (fluid)

1 fluid ounce (2 tablespoons) = 30 mL
4 fluid ounces (1/2 cup) = 125 mL
8 fluid ounces (1 cup) = 250 mL
12 fluid ounces (1 1/2 cups) = 375 mL
16 fluid ounces (2 cups) = 500 mL

WEIGHTS (mass)

1/2 ounce = 15 g
1 ounce = 30 g
3 ounces = 90 g
4 ounces = 120 g
8 ounces = 225 g
10 ounces = 285 g
12 ounces = 360 g
16 ounces = 1 pound = 450 g

DIMENSIONS

1/16 inch = 2 mm
1/8 inch = 3 mm
1/4 inch = 6 mm
1/2 inch = 1.5 cm
3/4 inch = 2 cm
1 inch = 2.5 cm

OVEN TEMPERATURES

250°F = 120°C
275°F = 140°C
300°F = 150°C
325°F = 160°C
350°F = 180°C
375°F = 190°C
400°F = 200°C
425°F = 220°C
450°F = 230°C

BAKING PAN AND DISH EQUIVALENTS

Utensil	Size in Inches	Size in Centimeters	Volume	Metric Volume
Baking or Cake Pan (square or rectangular)	8×8×2	20×20×5	8 cups	2 L
	9×9×2	23×23×5	10 cups	2.5 L
	13×9×2	33×23×5	12 cups	3 L
Loaf Pan	8½×4½×2½	21×11×6	6 cups	1.5 L
	9×9×3	23×13×7	8 cups	2 L
Round Layer Cake Pan	8×1½	20×4	4 cups	1 L
	9×1½	23×4	5 cups	1.25 L
Pie Plate	8×1½	20×4	4 cups	1 L
	9×1½	23×4	5 cups	1.25 L
Baking Dish or Casserole			1 quart/4 cups	1 L
			1½ quart/6 cups	1.5 L
			2 quart/8 cups	2 L
			3 quart/12 cups	3 L